A portion of all sales will be donated to
World Central Kitchen—a national nonprofit started by
Chef José Andrés and his wife Patricia that uses "the power
of food to nourish communities and strengthen economies
through times of crisis and beyond."

www.wck.org

2021 Jeremy Cooper and Andy Klausner

Designer - Chris Treccani www.3dogcreative.net
Illustrator - Alice Calder
Editor - Cortney Donelson

Blog
www.cocktailhourmeets.com

Instagram
CocktailHourMeets

Facebook Group
Cocktail Hour Meets

ISBN 978-0-578-89973-2   Paperback
ISBN 978-0-578-89974-9   ePub

Cocktail Hour Meets...
L'APÉRO

A celebration of French wines, food,
and journeys of the past, amidst
hope for the future.

Because even when you
don't know what day it is,
there's still cocktail hour!

Jeremy Cooper
Andy Klausner

Table of Contents

Foreword   7

Paris   **10**
- Ginger-Absinthe Champagne Cocktail   12

Alsace   **14**
- Tarte Flambée (aka Flammekueche)   16

Burgundy   **18**
- Puff Pastry with Duck Confit, Pear, Fennel, and Brie   20
- Salmon Croquettes   22
- Gougères   24

Beaujolais   **26**
- Mushroom and Bayonne Ham Quiche   28

Rhône   **30**
- Citrus & Herb Marinated Olives   32
- Andalusian Gazpacho   34
- Herb & Lemon Grilled Quail   36

Provence   **38**
- Cuisses de Grenouilles à la Provençale   40
- Steak Tartare on Baguette   42

Corsica   **44**
- Roasted Red Pepper Pesto   46

Languedoc & Roussillon   **48**
- Chilled Spring Pea Soup with Lardon and Rosemary Cream   50
- Aubergines au Gratin à la Languedocienne   52
- Potato Galettes with Saffron Aïoli   54

South-West	**56**
● Black Truffle & Mushroom Risotto Arancini	58
Bordeaux	**60**
● Grilled Octopus in a Sauce Exotique	62
● Filet Mignon on Potato-Leek Crisps with Mushrooms	64
● Duck Rillettes on Baguette	66
● Fennel and Carrot Confit	68
Loire	**70**
● Tuna Tartare in Sesame Ginger Sauce	72
● Crab Cakes with Remoulade	74
● Three-Cheese Spinach Quiche	76
Calvados	**78**
● Veal Scaloppine Medallions with Calvados Sauce on Baguette	80
Champagne	**82**
● Petite Lamb Chops with `Nduja and Raw Honey	84
● Crab and Cucumber Canapés	86
Epilogue	*89*
About the Authors	*93*

Recipes paired with:

● Red Wine   ● Rosé Wine   ● White Wine   ● Brandy   ● Cocktail

Foreword

Cocktail Hour Meets . . . L'APÉRO allows us to share our love of France through the country's wines and cuisine under the evening ritual of *l'apéro*. It also affords us the opportunity to relive and share memories of trips we've taken to the country, covering every major wine region save for Corsica (and we couldn't exclude this wine tradition so unique within France). This latest installment of *Cocktail Hour Meets* has unquestionably been a sanity-saving labor of love as we enter year two of the pandemic!

But first, we need to take a step back, because many of you have probably never heard the term *l'apéro*; we certainly were not familiar with the actual term until we started research for the book (though all too familiar and appreciative of the concept and lifestyle). A shortening of the term *aperitif, l'apéro* is a uniquely French affair. It is the part of the day when the French convene for a drink over a cocktail or wine and small plates. There is always a variety and abundance of food, simple and unfussy, ready to enjoy so no one is stuck in the kitchen. A little later than our cocktail hour, it is typically after 6 p.m., and it is never done alone. There is no exact American equivalent, really.

Having not spent too much time in French homes, our experience over the years of *l'apéro* has been slightly different. As you will read in the book, we have been fortunate to eat at a number of the best and most iconic restaurants throughout France, some located in chateaux or grand estates. The tradition in many of these settings is to ease into the multi-course dining experience outside on a terrace or in an elegant lounge.

As you relax with a glass of wine or aperitif, the dinner menu is presented to peruse at your leisure. Importantly, throughout this time, a number of hors d'oeuvres are presented— sometimes all at once, other times in procession. Regardless, we have always loved this way of starting our evening—both in France and while working on this book.

While, traditionally, *l'apéro* is shared with as many friends as possible (the more the merrier!), given the pandemic-nature of circumstance, ours have been for two.

As stated in the first books of the series (*Cocktail Hour Meets . . . A PANDEMIC and Cocktail Hour Meets . . . A PRESIDENTIAL ELECTION*), which present a series of cocktail recipes, our passion is truly in wines (Jeremy is a level one sommelier). So, taking that passion and mixing it up with cooking and travel, we conceived our own version of *l'apéro*.

Depending on your point of view, there are essentially 11 major wine regions in France. In concepting this book, we realized that we have been fortunate enough to travel to 10 of the 11, having yet to visit Corsica as mentioned above (but we do have a dear friend from there if that counts!). Eleven wine regions . . . and we threw Calvados in just for good measure after poring through old photo albums for inspiration.

Now then: 12 regions. Of course, some regions have so many varietals and styles that we could not just showcase one wine for the region. So, this book will feature 24 wines (and one brandy). Our journey begins in Alsace, we travel roughly clockwise around the country, and end with a toast (or two) from Champagne! For each of the 25 experiences, we created our own version of *l'apéro* with foods from the region, and we include one food recipe as well. And there is even a little surprise before we start our journey.

We have, of course, taken our own liberties along the way. Some of the foods might not traditionally be included in *l'apéro*, but we wanted to showcase some favorite French dishes, many of which bring back memories of our visits to each region. And since we make the rules, and Jeremy doesn't like to follow rules, we may occasionally sneak in a non-French food that pairs well with a particular wine (and some of the recipes might not be so simple). Consider this a Midwestern-slanted Texas version of the French tradition.

We hope that you enjoy this trip with us!

(All of the wines featured were purchased at a local liquor store in Dallas, so they should be relatively easy to find. Jeremy didn't obsess with vintages or even specific producers most of the time, but rather on finding wines typical to the region. While the guiding principle was to keep each bottle under $30 (taking advantage of sales and discounts, of course), this really wasn't possible in Burgundy and Champagne . . . and, as you'll understand from our memories from the Rhône Valley, we did have a specific grower in mind, and that required upping the budget a bit.)

Paris

While this book focuses on individual wine regions, we simply couldn't ignore the capital—the City of Lights. Most of our trips began or ended in Paris. We survived Y2K in Paris, and many special birthdays have been, and will continue to be, celebrated in Paris.

There are so many positive memories. The food. Our experiences run the gamut, from Michelin-starred restaurants, including dinner at Alain Ducasse au Plaza Athénée (still the most expensive meal we have ever had) and lunch at Taillevent, to our favorite brasserie (Bofinger near the Bastille), to döner kebabs in the Marais. Long lunches at cafés in the 8th. Or the time we treated ourselves to a stay at the Ritz (during Fashion Week!) and ordered steak tartare from room service (prepared to our specifications in our room by two tuxedoed attendants while we watched in our robes).

The museums. Multiple trips to the Louvre, the Musée d'Orsay, Le Centre Pompidou (with its multiple street performers in the plaza outside), the Rodin. Shopping. Neckties (when we still wore them) and a complete silver setting from Hermès . . . back when the USD was strong! Strolls down St. Germain. The artful food and great chocolates at Fauchon at Place de la Madeleine.

And the time we took our young son on his first trip overseas. Eating a very messy chocolate crepe, gazing up at the Eiffel Tower, showing him the Mona Lisa and Venus de Milo, lunch at Maxime's, him literally skipping along the streets of Montmartre. Naively listening to the hotel concierge's recommendation that taking him to the dinner show at the Moulin Rouge cabaret (our table was nearly on the stage and he caught a feather from the boa of a topless performer) was age-appropriate (he was sworn to secrecy until high school graduation). A day trip to Versailles.

And, of course, we consumed many phenomenal wines along the way. Our day-drinking rule does not apply to vacations, resulting in many long lunches followed by afternoon naps.

But enough about Paris. Let's start our wine tour—but, true to the tradition of *Cocktail Hour Meets*, a cocktail and a recipe to commemorate Paris.

Paris

Ginger-Absinthe Champagne Cocktail

LES INGRÉDIENTS
½ ounce absinthe
½ ounce freshly squeezed orange juice
½ ounce freshly squeezed lime juice
¼ teaspoon sugar
1 (1 ½ inch) piece of ginger, peeled and thinly sliced
Brut Champagne, to top
Lemon twist, to garnish

LA PRÉPARATION

1 For the ginger syrup: Bring sugar, ginger, and a ¼ cup of water to a boil in a small saucepan. Reduce the heat to maintain a gentle simmer and cook until the syrup reduces to ¼ cup—about 6 minutes. Strain ginger syrup through a fine sieve and discard the ginger. Chill ginger syrup.

2 For the cocktail: Pour absinthe, ginger syrup, orange juice, and lime juice into a shaker with ice and shake vigorously to combine and chill. Strain into flute and top with Champagne. Garnish with lemon twist.

Pairing for *l'apéro*:
*Plateau de Fruits de Mer with:
Yellowtail sashimi, Poached lobster claws and tail,
Snow crab Legs, Bluepoint oysters,
Jumbo prawns, Homemade tartar and cocktail sauces*

Wine Region - Alsace

We have always had a love of gewürztraminer and pinot gris from Alsace, and the foods that they pair with. When we had the opportunity several years back to explore the region, Jeremy immediately reached out to industry contacts to arrange for a visit to the winery and vineyards of one of our favorite producers—Trimbach. What was supposed to be a casual visit turned into a full day of touring, highlighted by a tasting and lunch with Pierre Trimbach, the great-great-great (or great-great) grand-something (nephew or grandson) of the founder (1626)! It was a day that we'll never forget.

Historically and gastronomically, Alsace straddles France and Germany. This combination comes to life in the architecture, cuisine, and primary grape varietals of the region (although Alsace produces at a considerably higher alcohol content than Germany . . . another reason to love Alsace!). With its galaxy of Michelin stars, we ate our way through the countryside and discovered *tarte flambée* with a pitcher of the house gris at an outside café in the historic center of Strasbourg along the river Ill before dining in the elegance of Le Crocodile on our final night. And let's not forget lunches at Hostellerie La Cheneaudière, where we stayed out in the forest. Each day's special was a unique presentation of sole—memorable to this day.

Fast-forward to 2015 in NYC where Daniel Kreuther (arguably the second most famous Alsatian chef in the U.S.) opened his eponymous temple to his native cuisine. Jeremy has an annual tradition with his best friend from business school which they call their "Irresponsible Holiday Lunch." It is a lunch that should take place midweek in the month of December at an expensive restaurant, and is a multi-course, multi-bottle event that never lasts fewer than two and a half hours. That year's lunch started with a bottle of their finest *Crémant d'Alsace* . . . and continued from there.

Wine Region - Alsace

Tarte Flambée (aka Flammekueche)

LES INGRÉDIENTS

¼ cup crème fraîche
⅓ cup fromage blanc
⅛ teaspoon freshly grated nutmeg
1 teaspoon kosher salt, more to taste
Freshly ground black pepper, to taste
1 ¾ cups all-purpose flour, plus more for dusting
3 teaspoons baking powder
4 teaspoons olive oil
2 large egg yolks
2 strips thick-cut smoked bacon, finely diced (about ⅔ cup)
½ cup finely chopped white onion

LA PRÉPARATION

1 If you have a pizza stone, place it on the middle rack of your oven, top with a baking sheet, and heat the oven to 425°. (If, like us, you don't have a pizza stone, just place the baking sheet on the oven rack.)

2 In a medium bowl, combine crème fraîche, fromage blanc, 1 teaspoon of olive oil, nutmeg, ½ a teaspoon of salt, and the pepper. Set aside while you make the dough.

3 In a separate medium bowl, whisk to combine flour, baking powder, and remaining ½ teaspoon of salt. In a small bowl, whisk to combine olive oil, egg yolk, and ½ a cup of water. Add to dry ingredients and use a fork to combine until it creates a shaggy dough. (NOTE: This dough recipe is a bit of a shortcut to avoiding dealing with yeast.)

4 Turn the dough out onto a floured surface and knead for 1 minute until the dough is uniform and elastic. (Flour your hands thoroughly to keep the dough from sticking.) Roll out to a 10-to-12-inch round, then transfer to a large square of parchment paper.

5 Spread fromage blanc mixture evenly over the dough, leaving a ½ inch border along the edges. Sprinkle bacon and onions over fromage blanc. Carefully remove hot pizza stone or baking sheet from oven and transfer, still on parchment paper, to cutting board or serving platter.

6 Bake until top is beginning to brown and sides are golden and crispy—about 20 minutes. Carefully remove hot pizza stone or baking sheet from oven and transfer the tarte still on parchment paper. Serve warm.

Trimbach, Pinot Gris Reserve, Ribeauville, 2016

Bright fruit with a touch of pear honey and structured acidity.

Pairing for *l'apéro*:
Tarte Flambée
Soft pretzels with grainy mustard
Sauerkraut with apples
Muenster cheese with smoked sausage
Cornichons

Wine Region - Burgundy

We have three distinct highlights from our visit to Burgundy. The first was (thanks again to Jeremy's industry contacts) a private tour and tasting at Maison Louis Latour . . . during the harvest! We had experienced a harvest before in the Veneto, and it is always exhilarating to witness and experience the energy and magic firsthand; especially in the grand cru vineyards of Corton.

The other two highlights involved unforgettable meals and stays at the properties of two classic and renowned French chefs: Georges Blanc and Bernard Loiseau. The villages where they are situated would be less than an afterthought if not for the true embodiment of three stars in the Michelin guide: exceptional cuisine that is worth a special journey.

The village of Vonnas over the years has been transformed into a gourmet destination with the Village Blanc housing the luxury inn and spa . . . and the Restaurant Georges Blanc. The area is known for its Bresse (AOC) chicken, declared by the legendary Brillat-Savarin as "the queen of poultry, the poultry of kings." Legally produced only in the designated area of Bresse, these majestic birds evoke the tri-color with red comb, white feathers, and blue legs.

The experience, while highly curated, was authentic and wonderful. It was raining when we drove in that first afternoon, so we were able to wander (snoop) around the kitchen and dining room as staff began to arrive and prepare for the nightly dance. (Andy had actually been here before, but that is another lifetime ago and another story.) George Blanc has since retired, replaced by one of his sons.

The town of Saulieu is home to Bernard Loisseau's Restaurant La Côte d'Or-Le Relais, the next stop in our exploration of Burgundy. Something that stands out (aside from encountering our first curated bottled water list) is an older couple from Philadelphia seated at the table next to us at dinner . . . with a small dog. As we made our way through the multiple courses and pairings and into the digestif, we learned that they visited Loisseau every year with the dog, with exact travel dates dependent on when flights were available to accommodate the dog in the cabin!

While the establishment still exists, Bernard Loiseau died by suicide in 2003 amid newspaper rumors that he was going to lose his coveted third Michelin star.

Wine Region - Burgundy

Puff Pastry with Duck Confit, Pear, Fennel, and Brie

LES INGRÉDIENTS

1 sheet puff pastry, defrosted
1 duck leg confit, skin removed, meat chopped
1 small bulb fennel, chopped, plus fennel fronds, chopped for garnish
1 large firm pear, peeled and chopped
1 teaspoon thyme leaves, minced
1 clove garlic, minced
1 tablespoon olive oil
5 ounces brie cheese, rinds included, chopped into ½ inch pieces
1 tablespoon sherry vinegar

LA PRÉPARATION

1 Mix the fennel, pear, thyme, garlic, and olive oil in a large bowl and season with salt and pepper. Place on a baking sheet in an even layer and roast for 15-20 minutes in a 400° preheated oven. Stir 2–3 times. Reduce oven to 375° after first stir and leave at 375° for Step 4.

2 Place chopped duck confit and sherry vinegar into a mixing bowl and add the fennel mixture. Stir to combine. Taste, and season again with salt and pepper if necessary.

3 Roll out thawed puff pastry on a floured work surface into a 12-inch square. Cut the puff pastry sheet into 24 equal pieces. Press each piece into a mini muffin tin, making a small cup.

4 Place 1 square of brie cheese in each mini muffin cup. Add 1 ½ teaspoons of the duck, sherry, pear, and fennel mixture. Bake for 20 minutes. Let cool for 5 minutes before serving. Garnish with fresh thyme leaves and fennel fronds.

Domaine L. Chatelain, Chablis, 2017

Clean bouquet of green apple and pear, unoaked, acidic, and very minerally.

Pairing for *l'apéro*:
Puff pastry with duck confit, pear, fennel, and brie
Smoked trout with caperberries and honey mustard
Fromage blanc blended with raw honey and extra virgin olive oil
Tunisian orange-almond cake

Wine Region - Burgundy

Salmon Croquettes

LES INGRÉDIENTS
½ cup white wine
3 tablespoons Old Bay seasoning
1 tablespoon plus 1 teaspoon kosher salt
1 pound boneless salmon fillet
1 ½ cups dried breadcrumbs
3 tablespoons unsalted butter, melted
4 scallions, finely sliced
1 small yellow onion, finely chopped
2 eggs, beaten
Juice of 1 lemon
Canola or grapeseed oil for frying

LA PRÉPARATION

1. Combine 4 cups of water, wine, 2 tablespoons of Old Bay, and 1 tablespoon of salt in a skillet and bring to a boil over high heat. Add salmon fillet skin-side down, turn off the heat, cover, and let salmon cook gently in the hot liquid for 10 minutes. Transfer salmon to a plate (salmon should still be rare in the middle).

2. Peel off and discard salmon skin. Break salmon into small pieces and place pieces in a large bowl. Add the remaining Old Bay and salt, along with the breadcrumbs, butter, scallions, onions, eggs, and lemon juice. Stir until just combined (you still want small chunks of the fish) and refrigerate for a ½ hour.

3. Form mixture into 2-inch patties and refrigerate for at least 1 hour or overnight (covered) on a parchment-lined baking sheet.

4. Add about ½ inch of oil to a large, heavy frying pan and heat to medium-high. Add croquettes to hot oil (go in batches if necessary to avoid crowding) and fry until golden brown (about 3 minutes per side), turning only once. Serve hot.

Domaine de la Renaissance "Les Reclots", Premier Cru, Rully, 2017

Golden straw color with restrained tree fruit scent and lightly toasted oak finish.

Pairing for *l'apéro*:
Salmon canapès three ways: salmon croquettes, smoked salmon on crispy crushed potatoes, gravlax on cucumber
Vegetable purses
Fermented vegetables
Cheese sticks

Wine Region - Burgundy

Gougères

LES INGRÉDIENTS
For the puffs:
1 ¼ cup water
¼ pound unsalted butter
½ teaspoon salt
1 cup flour
4 large eggs
½ pound finely grated Gruyère cheese

For the glaze:
1 egg yolk
1 teaspoon water

LA PRÉPARATION

1 Preheat the oven to 400°. Lightly grease a baking sheet.

2 Heat water, butter and salt in saucepan over medium heat. Once butter has melted, raise heat and bring to a boil and then remove saucepan from heat. Add the flour and mix well with a wooden spoon. When you have a smooth dough, place the saucepan over a low heat and stir constantly until the mixture no longer sticks to the bottom—about 2 minutes. Remove from heat.

3 Add the eggs one by one, stirring vigorously to incorporate each egg before adding the next (and before it starts to cook). Stir in the grated cheese. Take your time to fully distribute the eggs and cheese.

4 Using a tablespoon, place heaping mounds of dough on the baking sheet, leaving plenty of space around each mound to allow room for the puffs to expand.

5 Place the egg yolk and water in a small bowl and whisk to make the glaze. Using a pastry brush, paint each mound with a little glaze.

6 Bake for 5 minutes with the oven door slightly ajar, then close the door and continue baking until golden brown—another 12–18 minutes. Serve warm.

Domaine Chevillon-Chezeaux, Haute-Côte de Nuit, 2018

Fresh black cherry nose, light tannin, and concentrated dark fruit.

Pairing for *l'apéro*:
Gougères
Escargots à la Bourguignonne
Pork pâté de campagne, baguette, cornichons

Wine Region - Beaujolais

The wine geek in Jeremy insists on letting you know that Beaujolais is *technically* a part of Burgundy but, given his love of Burgundy and despite his general disdain for Beaujolais (and the Gamay grape . . . and any wines employing carbonic maceration in general), we decided to break it out as a distinct region for the book.

For Jeremy's big 35th birthday, we visited Beaujolais and Rhône, which you will read about in the next chapter. For Beaujolais, a friendly importer graciously connected us with the team at Mommessin, located in a castle-fortress surrounded by vineyards and owned by the family for nearly 450 years. There had been a very heavy snow prior to our visit, and the castle and grounds were magical as we made a quick tour before whisking away to the dining room for lunch with the winemaker (a woman, uncharacteristically) to explore their cru Morgon and Saint-Amour wines with a perfectly-paired roasted chicken. We both gained an appreciation for what a truly well-made Beaujolais could be.

We stayed at the magnificent Château de Bagnols, built in 1217 in the heart of the wine land straddling Beaujolais and Rhône. Partly due to the weather and partly due to off-season, we were told as we checked in that we were the only guests of the Château for the first night of our stay . . . but not to worry, as all hotel services (including valet and 24-hour room service) would be at our disposal.

After a stroll through the snow-covered property, we got ready for our dinner in the restaurant, aptly named 1217. The vast dining room with its large, heavy chandeliers, a medieval feel, and an enormous carved stone fireplace, still managed an intimate feel. However, it was all ours that evening as the only guests. It was the royal treatment with a brigade of servers and a sommelier to tend to our every need. They had even built a raging fire just for us and sat us in front of it. Truly memorable.

Wine Region - Beaujolais

Mushroom and Bayonne Ham Quiche

LES INGRÉDIENTS

2 tablespoons unsalted butter
½ pound white mushrooms (sliced ¼ -inch thick)
Salt and freshly ground pepper
4 large eggs
¾ cup heavy cream
½ cup milk
3 ounces Bayonne ham, ¼-inch dice
1 cup shredded Gruyère (3 ounces)
2 sheets of all-butter puff pastry, thawed

LA PRÉPARATION

1 Pre-heat oven to 350°. In a large skillet, melt the butter. Add the mushrooms, season with salt and pepper, and cook over moderate heat, stirring occasionally until tender and browned—about 8–10 minutes. Let cool.

2 In a medium bowl, whisk the eggs with the cream, milk, ½ a teaspoon of salt, and a ¼ teaspoon of pepper. Fold the mushrooms, ham, and cheese into the egg mixture.

3 Roll out the puff pastry on a floured surface until about ⅓ larger in size. Cut pastry into three equal squares and place into the cups of a large muffin tin. Spoon quiche mixture equally into each cup.

4 Bake the quiche for about 25 minutes, or until it is lightly browned on top and the custard is just set. Transfer to a rack to cool for 15–20 minutes. Remove quiches from tin and serve.

Domaine Pardon "Cuvée Hugo", Fleurie, 2019

Wildflower and violet aromas with structured dark-berry flavor and a pretty ruby color.

Pairing for *l'apéro*:
Mushroom and Bayonne ham quiche
Crispy-skinned chicken drumettes with Dijon sauce
Muenster cheese, hard salami, and
Peppadew peppers

Wine Region - Rhône

As the 35th birthday celebration continued, Jeremy had arranged for us to meet the legendary winemaker Jean-Luc Colombo at his main estate vineyards in Cornas. Jean-Luc whisked us through the steep and snow-covered slopes of the vineyards in his Range Rover, passionately pointing out characteristics of the various plots of vines. An exhilarating start to a truly unique and special visit.

While we knew we were scheduled to have lunch with him, we were a little shocked when we arrived at his home, where we were greeted by his wife, Anne, and two large dogs. He had prepared a private tasting, which we began while he stoked the fire under an enormous stone hearth to grill the most beautiful ribeye steaks and Anne put the finishing touches on her *gratin dauphinois*. It was the apex of hospitality. Jeremy developed a camaraderie with Jean-Luc, and reconnected several times back in Boston and New York.

The other highlight of the Rhône journey was dinner at Troigros. It was snowing very hard that night, and we were debating whether to go or not (it was showing about an hour from our hotel on a printed Google map). We decided to give it a go.

What ensued was a two-and-a-half-hour drive through a winding mountain road that frayed our nerves and had us questioning our decision-making. We finally arrived. While we ended up being one of only two tables that made it in that night, the gracious staff quickly made us feel comfortable and cared for, coming in from the snow and cold. The food, wines, and service were world-class.

Of course, hanging over our enjoyment of dinner was the dreaded and snowy drive back to our luxurious solitude at Château de Bagnols. Noting this with the sommelier, he asked for a moment as he went to have an animated discussion with the maitre'd, returning with printed directions back to the hotel and noting that there was a highway only a few kilometers away! That opened the way to a (small) digestif before hitting the road.

(A previous trip to the Rhône Valley several years prior is worth mentioning in this space wherein we celebrated New Year's Eve dinner and indiscrimate hugs and kisses at the legendary Leon de Lyon, in the food-obssessd city of Lyon.)

Wine Region - Rhône

Citrus & Herb Marinated Olives

LES INGRÉDIENTS

2 cups Castelvetrano olives
2 cups Kalamata olives
1 cup sun-dried tomatoes
¾ cup really good extra virgin olive oil
3 tablespoons fresh lemon juice
3 tablespoons fresh orange juice
4 cloves garlic, chopped
2 tablespoons fresh parsley, chopped
1 tablespoon fresh rosemary, minced
1 tablespoon Herbs de Provence
2 teaspoons lemon zest
2 teaspoons orange zest
4 ½-inch pieces of lemon rind
4 ½-inch pieces of orange rind
½ teaspoon crushed red pepper flakes

LA PRÉPARATION

1 Combine all of the ingredients in a large resealable plastic bag. Seal and shake the bag.

2 Refrigerate for at least 2 days. Occasionally, turn the bag to re-coat the olives.

3 Pour olives and mixture into a colander and rinse briefly with cold water, preserving tomatoes, herbs and rinds with olives.

4 Refrigerate in a sealed container. Serve at room temperature.

Cave de Tain Nobles Rives, Crozes-Hermitage, 2019

Floral aromas with apricot and stone fruit flavors shine through dry minerality.

Pairing for *l'apéro*:
Citrus & herb marinated olives
Grilled asparagus with lemon buerre blanc
Peppered smoked salmon with caperberries
Camembert with toasted cashews and dried apricots
Crispy cheddar straws

Wine Region - Rhône

Andalusian Gazpacho

LES INGRÉDIENTS

3 garlic cloves, minced and smashed to a paste with ¼ teaspoon salt
3 tablespoons sherry vinegar
3 tablespoons olive oil
3 tablespoons water
¾ tablespoon cumin
½ baguette, toasted to croutons with Herbs de Provence
6 plum tomatoes, seeded, and chopped fine
1½ cups chopped, seeded, and peeled cucumber
1 cup finely chopped green bell pepper
¾ cup finely chopped red onion
6 tablespoons finely chopped fresh cilantro
Tabasco, salt, and pepper to taste

LA PRÉPARATION

 Combine all of the ingredients in a food processor and blend until the mixture is smooth. Season with salt, pepper, and Tabasco to taste. Refrigerate.

NOTE: Make at least four hours, and up until one day, in advance.

Chateau de Ségrès, Tavel, 2018

Deep ruby rosé with strawberry aromas and a spicy, well-structured mineral finish.

Pairing for *l'apéro*:
Andalusian gazpacho
Honeydew melon wrapped in Bayonne ham with
40-year Balsamic drizzle
Mitica cheese
Spicy Thai almonds and cashews

Wine Region - Rhône

Herb & Lemon Grilled Quail

LES INGRÉDIENTS

2 semi-boneless quails, legs and wings separated
1 teaspoon Dijon mustard
1 lemon, juice and zest
¼ cup olive oil
3–4 tablespoons chopped fresh mixed herbs; we used tarragon, chives, thyme, marjoram, and parsley.
Kosher salt and freshly ground black pepper

LA PRÉPARATION

1 Pat quail dry with paper towels. In a large bowl, whisk together Dijon, lemon juice, lemon zest, and olive oil. Stir in the herbs. Add quail, turning to coat in the mixture. Cover and set aside for about 15 minutes. (The quail can be marinated for up to 4 hours, if desired; just cover and refrigerate until ready to cook. Remove from refrigerator 30 minutes before grilling.)

2 Preheat a lightly-oiled grill to medium-high. Place the quail pieces on the grill, an inch or so apart. Grill for about 3 minutes, then carefully turn over and continue to grill until birds are just cooked through, about 3–4 minutes more. Remove to a platter to rest for 5 minutes.

Jean-Luc Colombo "La Louvée," Cornas, 2013

Intense fragrance of dark berries, tightly structured tannins, and ripe red plum.

Pairing for *l'apéro*:
Herb & lemon grilled quail
French onion soup
Roasted heirloom carrots with ras el hanout
and Dijon sauce
Istara Petit Basque cheese
and Rosette de Lyon

Wine Region - Provence

Our adventures in Provence were the result of two stops on the same Oceania cruise with some very dear friends that we detail further when we get to Corsica.

Upon disembarking at the Port of Marseilles, we visited the 14th-century castle of Châteauneuf-du-Pape, constructed under the papacy of Pope John XXII, the former Bishop of Avignon, as a residence in the north outside of Rome. We enjoyed a wonderful (wine-drenched) lunch in the shadows of the castle ruins. (While this is clearly in the Rhône Valley, we include it here because the journey from the ship took us through parts of colorful Provence.)

Next port of call was Monte-Carlo (don't worry—we'll return to Provence in a minute). Arriving at the harbor brought back memories from an indulgent visit many years ago when we stayed at the Hôtel de Paris, splurged on an incredible lunch at the Alain Ducasse jewel, Le Louis XV, overlooking the Place du Casino (and starting with Champagne service delivered to the table in a half-globe stocked with more than a dozen selections), enjoyed a lively dinner, the cabaret at Crazy Horse, and then Jeremy found roulette success at the Casino de Monte-Carlo across the plaza.

Back to the trip at hand . . . for years we had wanted to visit the ancient village of Èze, and it was a short taxi ride from Monte-Carlo. The town is literally built into the steep hills, and as you ascend, you pass through narrow, shop-

filled winding streets. The reward at the top is the hotel La Chèvre D'Or, with its effortlessly elegant restaurant overlooking the corniche.

We enjoyed an hours-long, rosé-filled lunch on the terrace with our friends, taking in the beautiful views and scents of the hills and the sea.

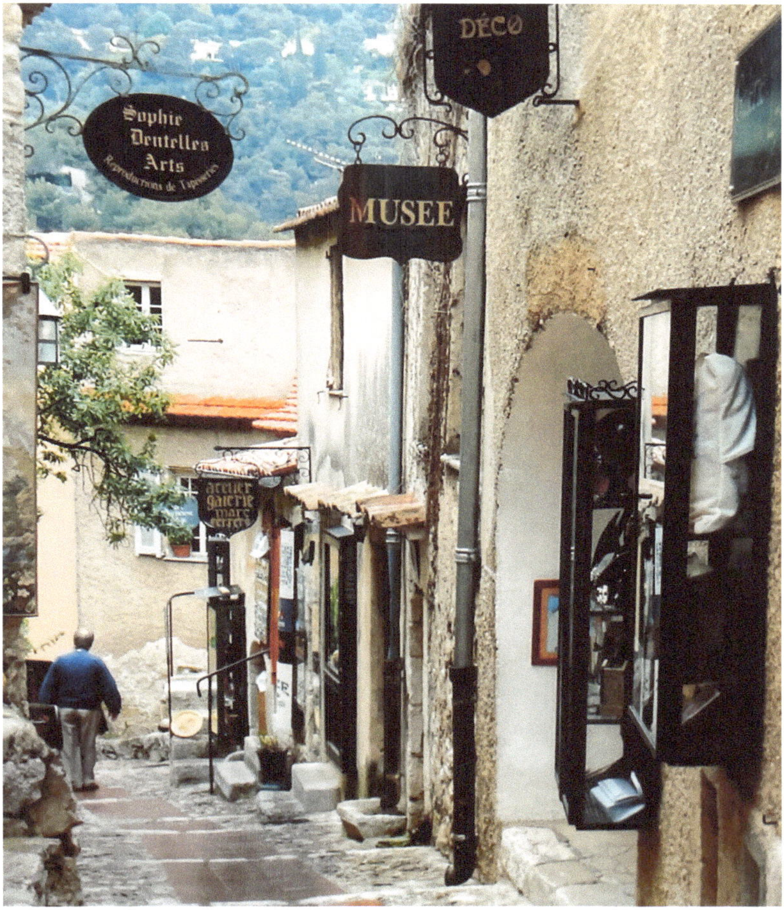
DÉCO
Sophie
Dentelles
Arts
Reproductions de Tapisseries
MUSEE

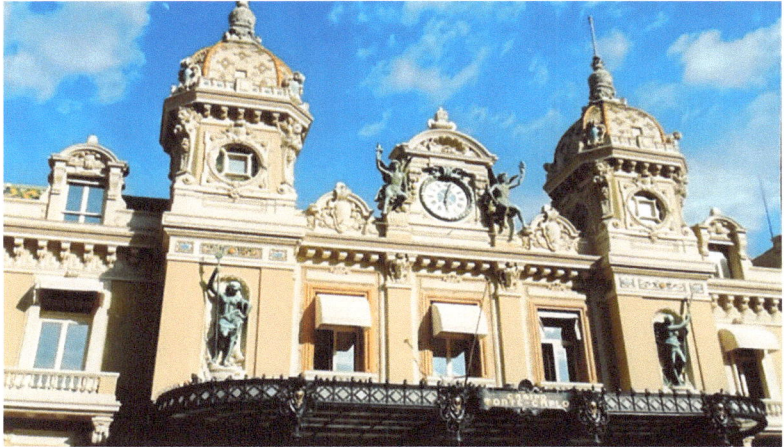

Wine Region - Provence

Cuisses de Grenouilles à la Provençale

LES INGRÉDIENTS
5–6 pairs of frog legs, separated
1 cup whole milk
2 tablespoons olive oil
1 clove garlic, chopped
2 teaspoons diced shallot
1 ounce white wine
1 teaspoon lemon juice
3 tablespoons capers, drained
8 olives, halved
6 grape tomatoes, halved
1 tablespoon unsalted butter
2 teaspoons chopped parsley
2 teaspoons chopped basil
Sea salt

LA PRÉPARATION

1 Separate each set of legs with a knife and soak in milk for 1-2 hours, refrigerated. When ready to cook, remove from fridge, pat dry with paper towels; let rest for 30 minutes at room temperature.

2 Sear the frog legs 2–3 minutes on each side with olive oil, chopped garlic, and shallots.

3 Add white wine and lemon juice and reduce for 2–3 minutes.

4 Add capers, olives, and grape tomatoes.

5 Add a tablespoon of butter to finish. Sprinkle with sea salt. Garnish with chopped parsley and basil.

Domaine de la Vivonne, Côtes de Provence, 2019

Pale salmon color with wild-strawberry fragrance and crisp, dry finish of mellow red fruit.

Pairing for *l'apéro*:
Cuisses de grenouilles à la provençale
Roasted vegetable focaccia
Olive tapenade
Salt & pepper breadsticks

Wine Region - Provence

Steak Tartare on Baguette

LES INGRÉDIENTS

2 large egg yolks
2 teaspoons Dijon mustard
4 anchovy fillets, finely chopped
2 teaspoons ketchup
1 teaspoon Worcestershire sauce
Tabasco
¼ cup really good extra virgin olive oil
1 ounce Cognac
1 shallot, finely chopped
3 tablespoons capers, rinsed
1/3 cup cornichons (about 10), finely chopped
6 sprigs of flat parsley, finely chopped
1 ¼ pounds fresh lean sirloin, trimmed and finally chopped
Freshly ground pepper
Griddled baguette slices

LA PRÉPARATION

1 Place the egg yolks in a large bowl and add mustard and anchovies. Mix well, then add the ketchup, Worcestershire, Tabasco, and pepper and mix well again. Slowly whisk in the oil, then add the Cognac and mix again. Fold in the shallot, capers, cornichons, and parsley.

2 Add the chopped steak and mix well, adding salt and pepper to taste. Serve immediately with griddled baguette slices.

Le Pont, Bandol, 2017

Deep garnet color with soft structured tannins and lightly spiced blackberries.

Pairing for *l'apéro*:
Steak tartare on baguette
Marinated vegetables — asparagus, artichokes. carrots, and eggplant
Pickled asparagus and fennel
Black and green olives
Almonds and cashews

Wine Region - Corsica

As we mentioned in the foreword, sadly, we have never been to Corsica. The closest we have come was on the cruise that took us into Provence, down to Sardinia, and on to Naples, which is just a few hundred kilometers across the Tyrrhenian Sea. We have given ourselves permission to wander a little from reality and, with that, share a favorite experience from Naples.

We planned a very special and much-anticipated leisurely lunch in the hills; planning to spend the cooler evening in Naples to indulge in the local limoncello and pizza. Once onshore, we hailed a taxi and traveled up a small mountain to the tiny town of Sant`Agata sui due Golfi and the two-star Michelin Ristorante Don Alfonso 1890.

Our driver, Aldo, was a pleasure, giving us his card and offering to pick us up after lunch (he actually wanted to have a lazy afternoon in the town, smoke some cigarettes, and down a few cappuccinos). We later arranged for him to meet us in our next port of call in Positano, where he acted as our tour guide for the day.

Once in Sant`Agata, we strolled around the little town with its central chapel before being greeted at the door of Don Alfonso and swiftly escorted to the terrace for—you guessed it—*l'apéro (aperitivo)* before lunch. After a relaxing glass of wine while perusing the menu, we were led to the rustic elegance of the dining room, where we mostly had the place to ourselves the rest of the afternoon. In selecting wines for the multi-course meal, we quickly hit it off with the sommelier, who actually suggested against some of the pricier selections Jeremy was considering and introduced us to a series of elegant pairings that were perfect with the produce from the restaurant's gardens.

At the conclusion of a decadent lunch, interspersed with conversations with the owners and chef, they offered to give us a tour of their ancient cheese cellars (the picture is of Jeremy navigating the steep and irregular stairs down to the sub-cellars). Even for a non-cheese-lover like Andy, the smell was incredible. As we came back up the stairs, we entered their boutique where, quite surprisingly, they had prepared a bag filled with fresh bread, pasta, and sauce of their famed San Marzano tomatoes for us.

Wine Region - Corsica

Roasted Red Pepper Pesto

LES INGRÉDIENTS

2 large red bell peppers, de-seeded and cleaned
1 large clove of garlic
1 tablespoon chopped Calabrian peppers
2 tablespoons pine nuts
½ cup loosely packed basil leaves
Salt and pepper to taste
3 tablespoons olive oil
Crostini, toasted or grilled

LA PRÉPARATION

1 Preheat oven to 400°.

2 Slice the red peppers into large pieces and place skin-down on a baking sheet. Drizzle 1 tablespoon of the olive oil over the peppers and sprinkle with salt. Place in the oven for 20–25 minutes until the peppers are soft and the edges are slightly transparent. The skin should also be slightly blackened.

3 While the peppers are in the oven, lightly toast the pine nuts in a pan over medium heat, shaking the pan frequently to keep from burning (pine nuts should just start to become fragrant and then be removed from heat).

4 Combine the red peppers, garlic, Calabrian peppers, pine nuts, basil, and 2 tablespoons of olive oil in a food processor. Blend until it has a nice, thick consistency. Season with salt and pepper.

NOTE: Can last for up to 2 weeks if refrigerated in an airtight container.

Domaine de Terra Vecchia, Alba di Diana, 2018

Soft black cherry and plum with hints of tar and dried herbs.

Pairing for *l'apéro*:
Crostini three ways: roasted red pepper pesto, prosciutto and goat cheese, and anchovy spread
Herbed mixed nuts
Olives

Wine Region - Languedoc & Roussillon

This trip was to celebrate Jeremy's 40th birthday, and the theme was the search for the perfect Cassoulet. But first, Paris. A fabulous lunch at Arpège on the Left Bank, where, as chef Alain Passard was making his rounds through the dining room, he saw the wine that Jeremy ordered (a splurge on a Grand Cru Chablis), and was delighted because he felt it paired well with the vegetable focus of the day's menu. Of course, we had to offer Chef a glass (which he quickly accepted with almost childlike joy), and he sat down to chat. The actual birthday dinner could not have been more different in setting: Le Pré Catelan, an old French Manor house in the Bois de Boulogne.

But we digress . . . time to leave the city in search of that perfect Cassoulet! We had our tickets for the TGV departing from Montparnasse shortly after noon the next day, so we bought some beautiful sandwiches and a bottle of Champagne for the 4-hour train to Toulouse.

Over the course of the trip, we consumed at least half a dozen cassoulets, from "light" (they say in air quotes) to rich and rustic and, while it is hard to say if we found the perfect one, it was an excellent study for which we were awarded a few extra pounds. We were able to buy the clay dish it is made in and from where it gets its name (cassole d'Issel), and some tarbaïs beans to bring home.

Beyond the cassoulet was the opportunity to explore the harsh, windswept mountains and craggy hills along which the ancient vines of grenache, cinsault, roussanne, marssanne, and so many other varietals which have been tortured for decades to produce the rich and minerally wines of the region, now really upping their game in quality.

A trip to the region wouldn't be complete without a visit to the medieval fortified city of Carcassonne where we had lunch (cassoulet) at La Barbacane in the historic Hotel de la Cité. Finally, we discovered Limoux—arguably the original producer of sparkling wine, but we can let the monks duke that out—where we happened upon a bizarre festival taking place in the town square with elaborate costumes, music, and the constant pop of the cork.

Wine Region - Languedoc & Roussillon

Chilled Spring Pea Soup with Lardon and Rosemary Cream

LES INGRÉDIENTS

- 1–2 ounces slab bacon, cut into 2–3 pieces
- 1 tablespoon extra-virgin olive oil
- 2 celery ribs, thinly sliced
- 1 onion, thinly sliced
- 1 leek, white part only, thinly sliced
- 5 cups chicken stock
- 2 rosemary sprigs
- 1 garlic clove, minced
- Salt and freshly ground, white pepper
- ½ pound fresh fava beans, shelled
- ¼ pound sugar snap peas, thinly sliced
- ¼ pound snow peas, thinly sliced
- 1 ½ pounds of fresh English peas, shelled
- ¼ cup flat-leaf parsley leaves
- 5 slices of extra thick smoked bacon
- 1 cup heavy cream

LA PRÉPARATION

1 In a medium soup pot, cook the slab bacon over moderate heat until browned and crisp, about 6 minutes. Transfer to a plate. Pour off the fat in the pot.

2 In the same pot, heat the olive oil. Add the celery, onion, and leek, and cook over moderately low heat, stirring occasionally, until softened but not browned, about 7 minutes. Add the chicken stock, the cooked slab bacon, 1 rosemary sprig, and a pinch each of salt and white pepper. Simmer until the vegetables are very tender, about 15 minutes. Discard the bacon and rosemary. Let mixture cool before pouring it into a blender and process until smooth.

3 Meanwhile, bring a medium saucepan of salted water to a boil. Add the sugar snaps and snow peas, and cook for 3 minutes. Add the English peas and cook for another 3 minutes. Add the parsley and fava beans; cook just until heated through, about 1 minute, and drain. Add the pea mixture to the blender and puree until as smooth as possible, adding a few tablespoons of the broth to loosen the mixture along the way. Carefully strain puréed pea mixture through a cheesecloth over a fine sieve, a few tablespoons at a time. Transfer and thoroughly combine the soup and the pea mixture in a large bowl. Place in a larger bowl of ice water to cool.

4 In a small saucepan, bring the heavy cream, garlic, and remaining rosemary sprig to a boil. Simmer over low heat until slightly reduced, about 5 minutes. Strain the rosemary cream into a bowl and let cool. Slice bacon into ½-inch lardons and fry until very crispy.

5 Ladle the chilled pea soup into bowls and drizzle with the rosemary cream. Place the lardons into each bowl or cup and serve.

Les Vignes de Bila-Haut, M. Chapoutier, Côtes du Roussillon, 2018

Bright citrus nose, mineral lime and tangerine with a hint of salinity.

Pairing for *l'apéro*:

Chilled spring pea soup with lardon and rosemary cream
Smoked trout with honey mustard
Smashed avocado and blood orange pulp with thyme on toasted baguette
Grilled spring onions with raw honey and garam masala

Wine Region - Languedoc & Roussillon

Aubergines au Gratin à la Languedocienne

LES INGRÉDIENTS

1 tablespoon olive oil
1 eggplant, peeled and diced
2 ripe tomatoes, seeded and diced
1 teaspoon tomato paste
3 tablespoons red wine
1 clove garlic, chopped

3 tablespoons breadcrumbs
1 tablespoon parsley, chopped
2 tablespoons grated parmesan
½ tablespoon Herbs de Provence
Salt and pepper to taste
1 baguette

LA PRÉPARATION

1 Pre-heat the oven to 400°. Sauté the eggplant and tomatoes in Herbs de Provence and garlic in the olive oil. After the mixture reduces and softens, about 10 minutes, add tomato paste and wine. Turn down the heat and cook until the wine cooks down, approximately 5 minutes..

2 Mix the breadcrumbs, parsley, and parmesan cheese in a small bowl.

3 Top the baguette with a tablespoon of the eggplant mixture and sprinkle the breadcrumb mixture over the top.

4 Place in the oven for 10 minutes or until lightly browned. Serve immediately.

Château de Villemajou, Gérard Bertrand, Corbières, 2017

Inky black cherry color and aroma with lightly tannic, spicy finish.

Pairing for *l'apéro*:
Aubergines au gratin à la languedocienne
Moroccan lamb köfte with spicy tomato sauce and yogurt
Sausage-stuffed fried olives with frizzled sage and preserved lemon
Morbier cheese

Wine Region - Languedoc & Roussillon

Potato Galettes with Saffron Aïoli

LES INGRÉDIENTS

Potato Galette:
2 baking potatoes
4 ounces ghee (clarified butter)
½ teaspoon kosher salt
½ teaspoon pepper
Chopped parsley to garnish

Saffron Aïoli:
½ teaspoon saffron threads
3 tablespoons lemon juice
3 garlic cloves, chopped
1 ½ teaspoons kosher salt
1 teaspoon Dijon mustard
3 large egg yolks
1 ⅓ cups canola or grapeseed oil
⅔ cup extra virgin olive oil

LA PRÉPARATION

1 Steam potatoes for 20 minutes in boiling water and then refrigerate until cold. Peel cold potatoes and grate into a large bowl. Toss with kosher salt and pepper.

2 Heat half of the ghee in large skillet for a few minutes over medium heat. Form grated potatoes into 3-inch-diameter disks, pressing firmly. Transfer disks into the skillet and press down with spatula to avoid crumbling. Makes about 10.

3 Cook over medium heat for 10–12 minutes until crispy on the bottom. Carefully remove the galettes to a plate. Add the remaining ghee to the skillet. Once hot, return the galettes to the skillet on uncooked side and cook another 10 minutes. Remove galettes and garnish with parsley.

Saffron Aïoli:

4 Crumble the saffron threads into a small bowl with lemon juice and let stand for 10–15 minutes.

5 Peel the garlic and crush it with the side of a chef's knife. Place the garlic in mortar along with a ½ tablespoon of salt and grind into a paste.

6 Place the lemon-juice mixture, garlic paste, 1 teaspoon of salt, mustard, and egg yolks into a food processor. Blend on low to start, while gently drizzling the oils (alternating the two). Sprinkle in 1 tablespoon of cold water. Finish on high, blending for 20–30 seconds. Will last for up to 2 weeks in the refrigerator.

Maison Limoux, Crémant de Limoux, Brut

Lemony notes with chalky apple and lively bubbles.

Pairing for *l'apéro*:
*Potato galettes with saffron aïoli
Smoked sablefish
Wasabi peas & Sriracha peas
Pâtes de fruits*

Wine Region - South-West

Having sated our quest for the perfect cassoulet in the Languedoc-Roussillon, the trip continued into the South-West region of the country. The first stop was in Cahors, a town on the Lot river known for its very elegant malbec (côt)-based wines. After a walk through the town and exploring the surrounding medieval ruins, we headed to our final destination of the trip.

It was Valentine's Day, and we had booked a room at the Relais & Châteax Michel Trama (housed in the former residence of the Count of Toulousse) in the town of Puymirol. We were welcomed in our room by a small carafe of Banyuls and some dried fruit and nuts. We strolled around the quaint medieval square, eagerly anticipating our meal in the Restaurant Gastronomique.

We enjoyed *l'apéro* by the fireplace where we were served a delicious concoction of Crémant de Limoux with chestnut liqueur. Having been warmed by the fire and the aperitif, we were escorted to the dining room where we noticed a mix of people staying at the hotel, as well as some locals to celebrate the big day (to which we really hadn't paid too much attention). Each table was decorated with some Valentines and special menus. But as we got to our table, we noticed that ours was plain. We (especially Andy) were a little taken aback that we were being treated differently than the rest of the patrons—but, to be honest, happy not to have the elegant table molested by St. Valentine.

It turns out that being "in residence" (and . . . non-traditional) was a win: they offered us the choice between the holiday menu or their renowned six-course black truffle menu, being just two-hours' drive from Périgord. This privilege seemed to raise a second collective eyebrow in the dining room as we were spoiled by Chef Trama, his wife/proprietress, and the whole dining room crew. Chef Trama kindly signed a menu for us on the way out.

We were rewarded not only with the menu (proudly displayed in the wine room), but also with a quick tour of the kitchen by Chef and access to a back door to the inn and private passage to our room.

Wine Region - South-West

Black Truffle & Mushroom Risotto Arancini

LES INGRÉDIENTS

4 cups low sodium chicken stock
3 tablespoons unsalted butter
Truffle salt and sea salt
1¼ cups arborio rice
½ cup grated parmesan cheese
2 ounces low moisture mozzarella,
  cut into ½-inch cubes
Grapeseed oil, for frying

1 ounce dried mixed mushrooms
1 large shallot, minced
Freshly ground black pepper
½ cup dry white wine
1 tablespoon black truffle spread
1 cup all-purpose flour
2 eggs, beaten
1 cup dry breadcrumbs

Your favorite marina sauce, for dipping

LA PRÉPARATION

1 Heat the chicken stock, 1 cup of water, and dried mushrooms in a small saucepan over medium-low heat. Cook until the mushrooms are soft, about 5 minutes. Remove the mushrooms and finely chop. Adjust the heat to keep broth hot but not simmering.

2 Melt the butter over medium heat. Add shallots, season with salt and pepper, and cook for about 3 minutes. Add rice and cook, stirring occasionally, until lightly toasted, about 3–5 minutes. Stir in mushrooms and wine, season with salt and black pepper. Bring to a simmer and cook, stirring constantly, until liquid is fully absorbed.

3 Add a ladleful of hot broth and simmer until the liquid is fully absorbed. Repeat adding broth in 1 cup increments, until the rice is al dente and the liquid is mostly absorbed, about 25 minutes. Stir in the parmesan and truffle spread. Spread out the risotto in an even layer on a baking sheet and let cool. Cover loosely with plastic wrap and chill 60 minutes until it's cold and firm. Line another baking sheet with parchment paper. Take a ¼ cup of cooled risotto and shape it into a ball. Insert a piece of mozzarella in the center, squeeze the rice closed around it, and roll it until smooth.

4 Place flour, eggs, and breadcrumbs in 3 separate bowls. Season each with salt and pepper. Bread arancini: coat one at a time in flour, then egg, then breadcrumbs.

5 Heat 1-inch of oil in a large, heavy-bottomed pot over medium heat to 350°. Fry a few arancini at a time, rolling occasionally to brown evenly, until golden and crispy, 5–7 minutes. Drain on a paper towel-lined plate, sprinkle with truffle salt.

Georges Vigouroux, Antisto Tradition, Cahors, 2016

Deep garnet color with soft structured tannins and lightly spiced blackberries.

Pairing for *l'apéro*:
Black truffle & mushroom risotto arancini
Grilled baguette with truffle honey and ricotta spread
Roasted heirloom beets with Herbs de Provence
Olive & herbs mixed nuts

Wine Region - Bordeaux

As it often goes, a big thank-you to the, now in flux, Club 5-C and all of its perks with Relais & Chateaux for making this visit special: a suite booking at the Château Cordeillan-Bages gave us exclusive access to a private visit and tasting at Château Lynch-Bages across the road.

We dined in the hotel's ambitious gastronomic restaurant striving to bring modern, global touches in design and cuisine to the traditional and regional produce and traditions. The wine cellar has one of the greatest collections of *grands crus classés* Bordeaux in the world (if you're into that sort of thing!).

From our base in Pauillac, we circled back to St. Estèphe and took a leisurely drive, crossing the Médoc and marveling at the grand châteaux along the way, much of the architecture familiar from the labels of their great wines. Most notable, the exotic design of Cos d'Estournel (Jeremy found a birth-year bottle at an auction site shortly after we returned home and put it down for #40—not a great vintage, but a great memory). We crossed into the village of St. Emilion and spent the rest of the day over lunch and poking into the various local shops and extensive wine stores.

One other memory that stands out is from the often-overlooked city of Bordeaux. Friends had strongly recommended that we plan a dinner in the gritty city center off the river and beneath the cathedral at La Tupina. It was rustic and authentic cuisine (technically) of the south-west; rich and delicious. Besides the ambience, food, and wine, there was an intriguing and very well-dressed French couple seated at the table next to us. The much younger blond wife (just for context— not for judgment) was decked out in her finest Chanel and Hermès. You can imagine our shock when her main course arrived—a whole *rognons de veau* (veal kidney), delicately—but steadily—seeping blood and juices as she sliced into it. She proceeded to devour every bite, proficiently employing pieces of baguette along the way, with elegance.

Probably not something you would ever see in the U.S. Her dinner partner must have noticed our marveling at this feat and raised a glass with a sly grin.

Wine Region - Bordeaux

Grilled Octopus in a Sauce Exotique

LES INGRÉDIENTS

3 pounds poached octopus tenacles
2 cups freshly squeezed lemon juice (about 12 lemons)
½ cup soy sauce
¼ cup red pepper flakes
1 cup ponzu sauce
1 cup saké
2 tablespoons unsalted butter
¼ cup minced cilantro (stems and leaves)
¼ cup peanuts, chopped

LA PRÉPARATION

1 Prepare a grill on high heat (or use a grill pan over high heat). Grill poached octopus until charred, but not burnt—about 4 minutes per side. Remove from heat. Slice diagonally into 1-inch pieces.

2 Combine 1 ¾ cups lemon juice, soy sauce, and red pepper flakes in a large bowl. Add octopus, stir to coat, and refrigerate for at least 1 hour (and up to 4 hours).

3 When ready to serve, remove octopus from marinade. Place in a large sauté pan with the ponzu sauce, sake, remaining lemon juice, and 1 tablespoon of butter. Cook over medium-high heat until liquid reduces by half. Remove from heat. Add the remaining butter and stir until melted. Serve garnished with cilantro and peanuts.

Les Hautes de Larrivet Haut-Brion Grand Vin, Pessac-Léognan, Graves, 2018

Lemony and lightly floral nose with full-mouth honeysuckle and mineral finish.

Pairing for *l'apéro*:
Grilled octopus in a sauce exotique
Artichoke parmesan spread with red chili crackers
Charcuterie of herbed goat cheese, hard salami, and sun-dried tomatoes
Marcona almonds

Wine Region - Bordeaux

Filet Mignon on Potato-Leek Crisps with Mushrooms

LES INGRÉDIENTS

1 pound filet mignon,
 cut into eight portions
1½ pounds Yukon Gold potatoes,
 peeled and thinly sliced
8 ounces leeks, white part only,
 thinly sliced
1 tablespoon grated parmesan
½ tablespoon fresh thyme, chopped

1/3 cup olive oil
10 ounces mushrooms, diced
2 teaspoons all-purpose flour
1 cup heavy cream, warmed
7 tablespoons butter
Salt and freshly ground black
 pepper to taste
8 baguette slices, toasted

LA PRÉPARATION

1 Preheat the oven to 350°.

2 Place the potatoes, leeks, and olive oil in a mixing bowl and season with salt and pepper. Gently toss to mix well. Transfer to a 6x9-inch baking dish and pat gently to form an even layer. Cover the dish with foil and bake in the oven for 1 hour and 15 minutes or until the potatoes are tender. Let cool completely, cover with plastic wrap, and chill. Increase oven heat to 375°.

3 Melt 2 tablespoons of the butter in a saucepan, and sauté the mushrooms over medium-high heat for about 5 minutes or until lightly golden. Add the flour and thyme and season with salt and pepper and stir well. Stir in the cream and keep warm.

4 Cut the potatoes into 2"x 2" squares. Transfer to a baking sheet, sprinkle with the parmesan, and bake in the oven for 10 minutes or until the tops are browned.

5 While the potatoes are cooking, season the filets with salt and pepper. Melt 1 tablespoon of the butter in a heavy frying pan over high heat. Sear the filets for 2½–3 minutes on each side, or to the desired doneness.

6 To serve, place a layer of potato-leek crisps on each baguette, top with the filet, and add the mushroom sauce.

Château La Fleur Peyrabon, Cru Bourgeois, Pauillac, Médoc, 2016 (Left-Bank)

Elegant floral nose, fresh but assertive blackberry notes with cedar, graphite, and light tannin.

Pairing for *l'apéro*:

Filet Mignon on potato-leek crisps with mushrooms
Grilled zucchini with rosemary, cracked pepper, and smoked sea salt
Comté with Bayonne ham and dried cherries
Toasted pistachios

Wine Region - Bordeaux

Duck Rillettes on Baguette

LES INGRÉDIENTS

- 1 whole duck breast and 1 duck leg
- 2 cups plus 2 tablespoons water
- 2 garlic cloves, halved
- 2 carrots, 1 cut into ¼-inch-thick slices and 1 finely chopped
- ¼ ounce (1 packet) unflavored gelatin
- 2 tablespoons finely chopped fresh flat-leaf parsley
- 2 tablespoons Armagnac
- 3 medium shallots, sliced
- 4 sprigs fresh thyme
- 1 large bay leaf
- 1½ teaspoons kosher salt
- ½ teaspoon whole black peppercorns
- Baguette slices, toasted

LA PRÉPARATION

1 Remove all visible fat and skin from the duck breast and leg. Discard, or save for rendering later.

2 Pat the duck breast and leg dry and season with salt and pepper. Place in a large frying pan and brown over moderate heat, turning once—about 8 minutes total. Transfer to a plate.

3 Add Armagnac to the pan and deglaze, scraping up any brown bits, until most of the liquid is evaporated. Add 2 cups of water, shallots, garlic, sliced carrot, thyme, bay leaf, kosher salt, peppercorns, and duck with any juices on the plate, and cook at a very low simmer, covered, for 1 hour. Remove duck and place on a cutting board to cool. Shred duck meat, then chop.

4 Pour broth through a sieve into a bowl, discarding solids (if the liquid measures less than 2 cups, add water). Return to a cleaned pan and add finely chopped carrot. Simmer, covered, until carrot is tender—about 5 minutes.

5 While the carrot is cooking, in a cup, stir gelatin into the remaining 2 tablespoons of cold water and let soften for 1 minute.

6 Stir softened gelatin into hot broth until dissolved, then stir in the duck meat, parsley, and salt and pepper to taste. Ladle into crocks (you'll have about 3 cups total) and chill, covered, until set—3 to 4 hours. Let stand at room temperature for 20 minutes before serving.

Fortin Plaisance, Cheval Quancard, Grand Vin, Saint-Emilion, 2017 (Right Bank)

Deep ruby with toasty black cherry and leather notes, light tannins, and dark fruit.

Pairing for *l'apéro*:
Duck rillettes on baguette
Pickled shrimp with lemons and onions
Sharp cheddar
Gougères

Wine Region - Bordeaux

Fennel and Carrot Confit

LES INGRÉDIENTS

1 small fennel bulb with fronds for garnish

2 carrots

2 cups olive oil

½ teaspoon cayenne

¾ teaspoon sea salt

¼ teaspoon coarsely ground black pepper

3 (3-by-1-inch) strips of lemon zest, thinly sliced

LA PRÉPARATION

1 Quarter the fennel bulb lengthwise, then very finely slice lengthwise. Shave the carrots with a vegetable peeler into very thin, wide ribbons.

2 Heat the oil with cayenne, salt, and pepper in a saucepan over low heat until just starting to sizzle.

3 Add the fennel, carrots, and lemon zest and cook gently, without simmering, stirring occasionally until the vegetables are tender—about 20 minutes. Drain the oil in a bowl (the seasoned oil can be used in dressings and marinades for about a week) and transfer the vegetables to another bowl to cool to room temperature. Drizzle 2–3 tablespoons of the oil onto the confit before serving.

Château Misselle, Sauternes, Graves, 2018

Golden hues with scents of honey and apricots; long and balanced, sweet finish.

Pairing for *l'apéro*:
Fennel and carrot confit
Foie gras de canard on baguette
with fig jam and fleur de sel
Roquefort
Smoked sturgeon
Grilled pineapple

Wine Region - Loire

This is one of the few regions where we didn't actually spend time at a winery or in vineyards. The highlight of this region are the many glorious châteaux that dot the countryside. Fortunately, it was shoulder/off-season so we had many of them to ourselves. We enjoyed the contrast between the majesty of the buildings (both interior and exterior) against the flea market-like atmospheres that abound outside many of them. Once you pay your entry fee, you have no choice but to walk through a labyrinth of vendors selling souvenirs, books, and snacks.

Throughout this book, we have recounted fortunate stories of grand hospitality provided at many of the places where we have stayed and dined. While it is impossible to remember the details of much of what you ate or drank 20+ years ago, hospitality is remembered and felt forever.

Another example of this hospitality took place at Le Grand Hôtel Lion d'Or in Romorantin-Lanthenay. This self-proclaimed Renaissance-style mansion was built in 1540 by the Lord of Montigiron, a friend of King Francis I. The property has operated variously as a luxurious hotel and restaurant since 1774, making it one of the oldest restaurants in the world.

We had booked one night in the hotel so that we could experience the restaurant and further explore the diversity of wines of the Loire. Unfortunately, midway through the meal Andy started to feel feverish and very unwell. He decided to go back to the room to lie down, but insisted that Jeremy finish the dinner (with several dessert courses still to come).

Jeremy decided to skip cheese and dessert. Knowing the situation, the waiter asked him if he would allow him to bring dessert up to the room. Of course, he said yes.

Jeremy came back to the room and told Andy that they were going to bring "a few things up." Promptly came a knock at the door, and two waiters with a table and trays laden with the complete cheese and dessert experience (as well as the remaining wine courses). They went about placing these throughout the room and up a small spiral of stairs at a far wall (and flowers, of course), wishing Andy a speedy recovery.

That was memorable.

Wine Region - Loire

Tuna Tartare in Sesame Ginger Sauce

LES INGRÉDIENTS

Tartare:

5 ounces of sushi-grade tuna, cut into small cubes
2 green onions, finely chopped
1 tablespoon toasted sesame seeds
½ an avocado, chopped into small pieces
½ cup diced cucumber
½ a handful of cilantro, chopped
½ tablespoon lime juice
Pinch of salt & pepper
Sriracha

Sauce

1 clove of garlic, minced
1 tablespoon grated ginger
1 spring onion, chopped
1 tablespoon soy sauce
½ tablespoon sesame oil
½ tablespoon rice vinegar
½ tablespoon honey

LA PRÉPARATION

1. Mix the sauce ingredients in a bowl and set aside.

2. Add the tuna, green onion, and ½ a tablespoon of sesame seeds directly to the bowl of sauce and mix until combined.

3. In a separate bowl, mix together the finely chopped avocado, cucumber, all but 2 pinches of the cilantro, lime juice, salt, and pepper.

4. Plate your tartare by using a circular ramekin. Place the tuna mixture in first, followed by the avocado mixture. Refrigerate for at least 30 minutes.

5. To serve, carefully flip the ramekin over onto a plate. Garnish with the remaining sesame seeds and cilantro. Drizzle Sriracha over top.

Domaine de la Chézatte
"Cuvée Gabriel", Sancerre, 2019

Limestone and flinty minerality with a lemon finish.

Pairing for *l'apéro*:
Tuna tartare in sesame-ginger sauce
Smoked salmon fillet with black peppercorns
and capers
Red pepper and artichoke bruschetta
Herb-rubbed young goat cheese

Wine Region - Loire

Crab Cakes with Remoulade

LES INGRÉDIENTS

Crab Cakes:

1 pound jumbo lump crab meat, rinsed and strained
1 habanero chile, seeded and diced
2 teaspoons freshly squeezed lime juice
3 teaspoons fresh cilantro, chopped
3 teaspoons breadcrumbs
1 egg
2 teaspoons mayonnaise
½ teaspoon kosher or sea salt, to taste
¼ teaspoon freshly ground black pepper, to taste
1 tablespoon butter
1 tablespoon olive oil

Remoulade:

¾ cup mayonnaise
2 teaspoons Dijon mustard
1 ½ teaspoons whole-grain mustard
1 teaspoon tarragon vinegar
¼ teaspoon Tabasco
2 teaspoons capers, chopped
1 tablespoon flat-leaf parsley, chopped
Salt and freshly ground black pepper, to taste

LA PRÉPARATION

1 Combine the crab meat, habanero, 2 teaspoons of cilantro, breadcrumbs, mayonnaise, egg, and lime juice in a large bowl. Season with salt and pepper. Form 6–8 crab cakes (can be prepared and refrigerated up to two days in advance).

2 Heat a large skillet over medium-high heat, melt 1 tablespoon of butter into 1 tablespoon of oil. Once it starts to sizzle, place crab cakes in pan without crowding (you may need to work in batches). Cook 3 minutes per side, or until golden. Top with sauce and remaining cilantro and serve.

3 *Remoulade:*
Combine all of the ingredients in a bowl and refrigerate for 30 minutes to 2 hours.

Saget Pères et Fils, Vouvray, 2019

Off-dry with floral aromas and sweet pear and honeysuckle.

Pairing for *l'apéro*:
Crab cakes with remoulade
Samosas with chutney
Naan
Peppadew peppers

Wine Region - Loire

Three-Cheese Spinach Quiche

LES INGRÉDIENTS
1 shortbread pastry crust (homemade)
6 ounces roughly chopped spinach
5 eggs
1 garlic clove, minced
1 tablespoon sour cream
¾ cup crème fraiche
¾ cup heavy cream
½ cup chèvre
½ cup medium-sharp cheddar
½ cup gruyère
Pinch of salt and pepper

LA PRÉPARATION

1 Preheat oven to 350°.

2 Beat the eggs, sour cream, crème fraiche, and heavy cream in a large bowl.

3 Add the garlic, spinach, cheeses (mixed evenly), salt and pepper.

4 Spread the mixture across a pre-baked pie crust.

5 Bake for 35–40 minutes or until the top starts to brown.

6 Serve while warm.

Le Pré Vaujour, Chinon, 2018
Fresh blackberry bouquet with light tannins and long finish with a hint of anise.

Pairing for *l'apéro*:
Three-cheese spinach quiche
Grilled shrimp with curry cocktail sauce
Fried cheese ravioli with spicy marinara
Pork pâté with dried cranberries

Wine Region - Calvados

As mentioned in the foreword, Calvados is not technically a wine region (it is known for its apple brandy instead), but we loved our visit to Normandy and we decided to add it to the book, not least of which for the significance of sacrifice made on its shores. Our visit was over New Year's, so we were actually there when the hard Euro currency officially came into circulation on January 1, 2002.

We stayed at a wonderful inn called La Ferme Saint-Simèon, located in Calvados and not far from the seaside town of Honfleur. Claude Monet frequented the hotel due to its setting and light from the Seine estuary. We had a convenient half-board rate at the hotel that included an indulgent breakfast and choice of lunch or dinner daily at the hotel's restaurant, perfect for the low-key nature of this stop. A notable feature of the lunch and dinner menu was the daily whole, fresh, local fish encrusted in salt. It was brought to the table, salt crust cracked, and then filleted and plated. Perfect.

The highlight of this region, to us, was the opportunity to visit WWII Normandy—the cemeteries, the fortified beaches, the memorials, and the museums. It is hard to forget the starkly contrasing visuals and sensation you feel visiting, first the American and Allied, and then the German and Axis, cemeteries. Taking in the remains of the battlements, with the cannons still in place, is a stirring reminder of the bravery of our soldiers.

Other highlights of the visit included an evening stroll through the holiday-lit streets of Honfleur, illuminated by strings of lights shaped like langoustines, as well as a New Year's Eve celebration at Restaurant Gill in nearby Rouen where we were welcomed as locals.

During the days, we made off-the-beaten-path stops at small family farms peddling their house Calvados brandies and discovering the tradition of *pommeau* before a meal (making it a part of our well-known Thanksgiving dinners back home). On New Year's Day, we loaded up for the drive to Paris, receiving our first Euro coins as change at a tollbooth . . . a new chapter to come.

Wine Region - Calvados

Veal Scaloppine Medallions with Calvados Sauce on Baguette

LES INGRÉDIENTS

4 tablespoons unsalted butter
2 tablespoons grapeseed oil
8 veal medallions, about ¼-inch thick, cut from the tenderloin
Kosher salt & freshly ground black pepper
1 shallot, finely chopped
2 teaspoons fresh thyme leaves, divided use
⅛ cup Calvados
½ cup hard apple cider
3 tablespoons beef broth
1 Granny Smith apple, cored and diced
⅛ cup crème fraiche
Grilled baguette slices

LA PRÉPARATION

1 Heat 1 tablespoon of the butter and 1 tablespoon of the oil in a large sauté pan over medium-high heat. Season veal medallions with salt and pepper; brown the veal in batches, if necessary, about 1 minute each side. Transfer veal to a plate and set aside.

2 Melt 2 tablespoons of butter in the same pan. Add shallot; season with salt and pepper. Sauté until shallot is just cooked through, about 6 minutes. Stir in 1 teaspoon of thyme, sauté about 1 minute more. Raise heat to high and carefully add Calvados; cook about 1 minute then add cider. Continue to cook until liquid is reduced by half then stir in beef broth. Reduce heat to medium and thicken. Add veal and any juices that accumulated on the plate back to the pan and simmer medallions for about 2 minutes to warm.

3 While shallots and veal are cooking, heat the remaining tablespoon of butter in a medium skillet over medium-high heat. Add the diced apple; season lightly with salt. Sauté until apples are soft, about 5–8 minutes. Remove from heat.

4 In the last few minutes of cooking, remove the veal and stir the cooked apples, crème fraiche, and remaining teaspoon of thyme into the mixture. Taste for seasoning, adding salt and/or pepper, if needed. Serve 1 medallion per baguette slice and top with a portion of the sauce.

Berneroy, Fine Calvados

Crisp, dry apple backbone with light alcohol to cut through the buttery richness.

Pairing for *l'apéro*:
Veal scaloppine medallions with Calvados sauce on baguette
Grilled lobster tail with limoncello buerre blanc
Hard salami and breadsticks
Butter madeleines

Wine Region - Champagne

We end our trip around France with a toast from Champagne and a thank-you for taking the journey with us.

We have been to this region twice and, given our love of Champagne and the fact that it is only a 90-minute drive from Paris, we now wonder why we haven't been back since 2001! On both trips, we stayed at the incomparable Domaine Les Crayères in Reims, where the restaurant was then helmed by Chef Gerard Boyer, flaunting three Michelin stars. The original Houses of Veuve Clicquot and Champagne Pommery are a short walk away, heading toward the gothic Cathedral of Reims.

The rooms at the Château are beautiful, and every service encounter thoughtful and impeccable. While it is hard to remember what was on the menu at Boyer more than 20 years ago, we just remember that the overall experience truly embodied the "5-Cs" of Relais & Chateaux: *Caractère, Courtoisie, Calme, Charme, et Cuisine.* (The only unhappy memory is that Jeremy was still recovering from a less-than-perfect wisdom tooth extraction which made chewing somewhat painful on the second visit.)

Les Crayeres is where we really were indoctrinated with the ritual of *l'apéro*, as each evening began on the terrace of the Château, overlooking the back lawn and gardens. Tuxedoed waiters glided effortlessly from guest to guest with bottles of the nightly *tête de cuvée* (the top wine of the producer), pouring by the glass. This was our first experience with the show-stopping Philipponat "Clos des Goisses"; it was a thrill to explore what was being poured each night. And, if not for a little too much wind on the morning of our planned balloon ride over the vineyards, our adventure would have begun on that very lawn (we had to relocate to the less-congested countryside to both begin and end the ride).

Other fond memories of the region included a private tour of the caves at Louis Roederer, a day trip to Épernay to explore the Disneyesque Moët et Chandon experience, and then a fabulous lunch on the terrace at Le Royal Champagne.

Wine Region - Champagne

Petite Lamb Chops with `Nduja and Raw Honey

LES INGRÉDIENTS

8 small lamb chops
4 ounces thinly sliced pancetta
½ cup Calabrian chili peppers in oil (2-3 tablespoons)
12 ounces sliced salami
2 tablespoons olive oil
¼ cup butter, room temperature
Raw honey

LA PRÉPARATION

1 Cook the pancetta over medium heat, tossing occasionally until it starts to crisp (4–5 minutes).

2 Remove the pepper stems. Place the peppers, salami, pancetta, and chili oil in a food processor. Pulse on and off until mixture is finely ground. Add olive oil and butter and process until smooth and spreadable.

3 Transfer 'njuda to a bowl, cover with plastic wrap, and refrigerate (8 hours to overnight).

4 Bring a grill to high heat and grill the lamb chops for 2 minutes, then turn over, spread 'nduja on the cooked side, and continue grilling for about 3 minutes for medium-rare. Serve with honey on the side.

Gervais Gobillard, Rosé, Brut, Hautvillers

Orange-tinged color with cherry and citrus notes with extended aging sur lie for backbone and a lingering finish.

Pairing for *l'apéro*:
*Petite lamb chops with `nduja and raw honey
Roasted scallions and heirloom carrots with Champagne vinaigrette
Brie with hazelnuts*

Wine Region - Champagne

Crab and Cucumber Canapés

LES INGRÉDIENTS
1 pound fresh lump crab meat
½ cup mayonnaise
2 tablespoons fresh chives
1 shallot, minced
Juice from ½ a lime
Sea salt, to taste
1 English cucumber
¼ teaspoon smoked paprika
Dill for garnish

LA PRÉPARATION

1 In a bowl, stir together the crab meat, mayonnaise, chives, shallot, lime juice, and salt.

2 Slice the cucumber thinly on a diagonal. Place a dollop of the crab mixture on top of each cucumber slice, sprinkle with the paprika, and garnish with dill.

Franck Bonville, Blanc de Blanc Grand Cru, Brut, Avize-Oger

Bone-dry with tight minerality and salinity delivered with an effusive bead.

Pairing for *l'apéro*:
Crab and cucumber canapés
Ossetra caviar service
Smoked sturgeon with caperberries
Brie with almonds

Epilogue

Thank you for joining us on this journey through France and taking the time to partake in *l'apéro*. As we went through old photo albums preparing to write the book, we not only relived some great experiences, but we were able to reflect upon how blessed we have been to travel and experience all that we have. (And we look forward to doing it again soon!) Andy also felt validation for his obsessive documentation of our trips.

We hope that you enjoyed the stories, recipes, and wine pairings. We also hope you understand that these tales were not a "humble brag" about these experiences, but rather, sharing them not only offered fond reflections for us but perhaps also will provide inspiration for our friends and readers as we find our "next normal." Of course, please feel free to contact us with any questions or for further details—you know that Jeremy loves to plan a trip or a convivial *apéro*!

We began work on this book in February 2021 and finished in May the same year. The process, like the past year and a half of the pandemic, had its ups and downs. We are cautiously optimistic and glimpse some light at the end of this tunnel. On the positive side, we were both fully vaccinated for COVID-19 by the end of April; we were finally able to host some friends (also fully vaccinated) for *l'apéro* over Easter weekend; Jeremy was able to drive to his hometown for Mother's Day weekend to see family for the first time since Christmas 2019; and, we were able to travel back to New York City in May to see old friends (and redeem credits from a canceled trip in 2020).

Of course, as we all know—and the pandemic further confirmed—things do not always go smoothly or as planned. We had to pause work on the book for ten days when a temporary illness caused Jeremy to go on a ten-day prescription of antibiotics that outright prohibited alcohol consumption and "discouraged" rich or heavy foods. And, not to be outdone, the temperature and humidity control in the wine room gave out and had to be replaced.

Early April also saw the first anniversary of our first Facebook post of a cocktail that launched fifty straight days of cocktails and our first book in the series, *Cocktail Hour Meets ... A PANDEMIC*. And the progression of our work portrays our overall mood. This first book was written in the early days of the pandemic, a period of intense anxiety as no one really had any idea how bad this thing was or how to even fight it. The first person we spoke to about the book said that we better rush to get it published so that it was still relevant. That was May of 2020.

The second book, *Cocktail Hour Meets ... A PRESIDENTIAL ELECTION* was a great diversion during an incredibly charged election period. Regardless of party affiliation, we think it is safe to say that the entire country was on edge. Just as with the first book, this one allowed an escape from *BREAKING NEWS*, taught us a lot about our great presidential tradition . . . and provided us an excuse to toast each other each evening and be thankful.

And now this book. It is a return to our true loves—food, travel, and wine. Yes, it is a look back at past trips, but it underlies our positive, albeit cautious, feelings about the future. We are talking about planning a trip later in the year, a blowout for sure! And it was so much fun incorporating food into the book because from day one, food and cooking have helped us get through this pandemic.

We hope that you enjoy the recipes and the stories and that you'll try a bottle or two (or three) of the wines, exploring new regions and varietals. And, as you partake in *l'apéro* with your friends and family, we would love to see pictures! As we have said throughout this pandemic, even when you don't know what day it is, there's still cocktail hour!

With that, a quote and a toast from Francis Bacon (the English Lord, not the genius painter): *Champagne for my real friends, real pain for my sham friends*. Cheers!

info@cocktailhourmeets.com

Fin

About the Authors

Andy and Jeremy currently live in Dallas, Texas, and have been together since 1997. When not working, or quarantined at home, they enjoy traveling, eating, cooking, entertaining new and old friends, and discovering and sampling new wines, tequilas, and whisk(e)ys. Feel free to reach out to either of them with questions or comments.

info@cocktailhourmeets.com

www.ingramcontent.com/pod-product-compliance
Lightning Source LLC
Chambersburg PA
CBHW040548010526
44109CB00055B/142